PLAY BETTER GOLF

HOW TO BREAK 90

The mental and tactical approach

Beverly Lewis

Illustrations by Ken Lewis

SMITHMARK

CLB 3177
© 1991 CLB Publishing,

This edition published in 1994 by
SMITHMARK Publishers, Inc.,
16 East 32nd Street, New York, NY 10016

SMITHMARK books are available for bulk purchase for sales
promotion and premium use. For details write or call the
manager of special sales, SMITHMARK Publishers, Inc.,
16 East 32nd Street, New York, NY 10016; (212) 532-6600.

Produced by CLB Publishing,
Godalming Business Centre, Woolsack Way,
Godalming, Surrey GU7 1XW

ISBN 0-8317-4038-8

Printed and bound in Malaysia
10 9 8 7 6 5 4 3 2 1

Contents

Beverly and Ken Lewis

Beverly Lewis became a professional golfer in 1978 and has twice been Chairman of the Women's Professional Golf Association. A PGA qualified professional since 1982, she has played in many major tournaments and is an experienced teacher. She has been a regular contributor to *Golf World* magazine in the United Kingdom for six years and is the only woman on their teaching panel. She has won two tournaments on the WPGA circuit but now concentrates on her teaching commitments.

Beverly is co-author of *Improve Your Golf* (published in the UK by Collins Willow, revised edition), and has written the other titles in the *Golf Clinic Series*. Her interests include music and playing the organ.

Ken Lewis trained at the Southend College of Art and then worked as a commercial artist. He has illustrated many golf books, working with players such as Peter Alliss, Alex Hay and Sandy Lyle. His projects include illustrating newspaper instructional features and strips by Greg Norman and Nick Faldo, and he works for *Golf* Magazine in the United States. His hobbies include building and flying his own aeroplane.

Introduction

This book aims first and foremost to help you make the most of your ability. I assume that you have been playing golf for some time, and know a reasonable amount about the basic way to swing the golf club. Applying your skill on the golf course is usually much more difficult than on a practice ground or at the driving range. In this book, I am going to help you to transfer your game from the practice environment out onto the course, so that you can make the most of your current skills.

The first few chapters deal with the technical aspects, which will help you offset your swing faults, or at least to work around them. Course strategy and planning are next and I explain how you should apply yourself practically on the course, and how you should plan your round.

I then cover the mental approach to the game. It is often said that the most important six inches in golf are those between your ears! The correct mental approach can save you many shots, but just like hitting good drives, it must be practised and applied correctly. You can learn how to maximize a good round or minimize a bad one – one of my pupils plays three holes in a later chapter, and I have given a good insight as to how thinking and planning could reduce his score. Knowing a few appropriate rules can also save shots or help you, so I have covered this aspect of golf, too.

During the many years that I played tournament golf, I was involved in many Pro-Ams, and despite my sound advice, so often players chose to play their way, only to make a nonsense of the hole. Whilst in a better-ball situation, gambling may occasionally be a worthwhile risk, with a card in your hand, reality must always be at the forefront of your mind. Playing golf well is a discipline, and, although it is your hobby in which perhaps you seek to escape from and forget the disciplines of life, with a little more worthwhile application you should be well on the way to breaking 90.

CHAPTER ONE

The right equipment can help you

Many beginners start playing golf with an inexpensive, and often an unmatched, set of clubs, but if you have reached the stage of being reasonably competent, and wishing to break 90, then it is possible that you may wish to upgrade your equipment. This does not mean buying the most expensive set in the shop – far from it. What it does mean is buying a set that suits you. In recent years, technology has improved golf club performance, and most professionals have a stock of trial clubs which you can test before you buy, so do invest some time before you buy new clubs. The following advice should also help you to know what to look for in a new set.

Which clubs are right for you?

Below is a table showing which swing weight and type of shaft suit different categories of players (Fig 1.1).

Swing-weight	C0-C5	C6-C8	C9-D2	D3-D5
Shaft	L	L or R	R	S or XS
Category of Player	Lady beginner and average lady player. Slow swing and hand action.	Strong lady and weaker man. Reasonable hand and club speed. Man may feel that a lighter club is easier to control and L shaft helps clubhead speed.	Strong lady and average man. Good hand action and clubhead speed.	Strong man. Very fast hand action and clubhead speed.

Fig 1.1. The various swing weights and shaft flexes available, and which category of player they suit.

Swing weight

Swing weight is the system of measuring the balance of a club, and refers to how heavy the club feels when swung. As you progress with the game, it is quite feasible that you will become stronger, and thus can play with slightly heavier clubs than those with which you started. However, always guard against playing with clubs that are too heavy. When you try out a club, it may be when you are feeling quite fresh, but remember that towards the end of your round, you may begin to feel a bit weary, and the clubs may start to feel too heavy, causing you to lose control.

Shaft flex

The main shaft flexes available are L (ladies'), R (men's regular), S (men's stiff), and XS (men's extra stiff), each one being progressively stiffer than the last. The lighter the swing weight, usually the more flexible the shaft. Nowadays there are so many new materials being used for shafts, such as graphite and boron, which are all designed to help you hit the ball further. Although these are usually more expensive than steel shafts, if distance is one of the factors lacking in your game, you may well feel that the investment is worthwhile.

Grips

The two main grip thicknesses are ladies' and men's, the former being thinner than the latter. However, many companies make a greater variety of grip widths, and you can always have an additional layer of adhesive tape under the grips to make them thicker. So what is the importance of the

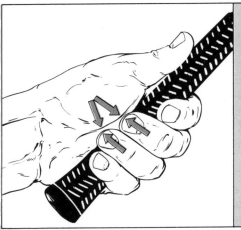

Fig 1.2. With the correct width grip the middle two fingers should be close to the pad at the base of the thumb.

grip thickness? Ideally when your left hand closes around the club, the tips of the middle two fingers should be quite close to the pad at the base of the thumb, which should enable you to have good control (Fig 1.2). Someone who slices may be using grips that are too thick, thereby preventing free hand action through impact. A player who hooks the ball could find that slightly thicker grips will stabilize over-active hands. Remember, however, that if you should alter your grip thickness, thinner grips make a club feel heavier to swing, whilst thicker grips will have the opposite effect.

Always keep your grips clean by washing them regularly with soapy water to keep them grease-free, and, if necessary, rough them up using sandpaper or a file. Grips do not last for ever, and once they become shiny and feel hard, then you will have to grip tightly to keep control, which will inevitably restrict good hand action. So if your grips reach this sad condition, then the time has come to have them re-gripped.

Club head choice

There are two main shapes of club head for irons, these being *blade* and *peripherally* weighted (Fig 1.3). The blade is the original shaped head where the weight is distributed fairly evenly. It is best used by the lower-handicap golfer or professional, who often likes the feel and look of this type of club. The *blade*-type head has a small optimum area of strike, known as the sweet spot. On the *peripherally* weighted club,

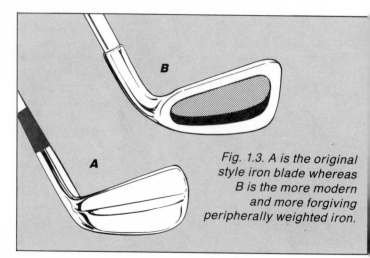

Fig. 1.3. A is the original style iron blade whereas B is the more modern and more forgiving peripherally weighted iron.

8

this is much larger, giving the less consistent higher-handicap golfer a much better chance of hitting the ball 'out of the middle'; thus it could be described as a more forgiving club. So the best piece of advice I can give you when buying clubs is to go for peripherally weighted ones, which most manufacturers now have in their range.

You can also buy woods that offer a similar advantage. Those that have heel and toe weighting have an enlarged sweet spot, as do metal woods, which consist of a metal shell filled with polystyrene.

The lie of the iron

When you address the ball the toe end of the iron should be just off the ground, so that through impact, where the wrists arch slightly, the whole of the sole will be in contact with the ground (Fig 1.4). If in your set the toe end sits up too much, the club is too upright, and can cause the heel to catch on the ground, closing the clubface at impact and thereby creating a pull or hook (Fig 1.5). If at address the whole of the sole touches the ground or the heel is off the ground, the club is too flat, and can cause the toe to catch the turf at impact, creating a push or slice (Fig 1.6). Check this on your current set, and especially if buying new irons. Most clubs can be adjusted to suit you, but be certain that this is done either by your professional or a good club maker. Because of the more rounded sole of a wood, and the fact that the ball is often hit from a tee peg when using them, the lie is perhaps less crucial, but do get the professional to check them as well.

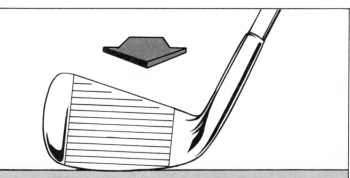

Fig 1.4. With the correct lie, the toe end sits just off the ground, encouraging straight shots.

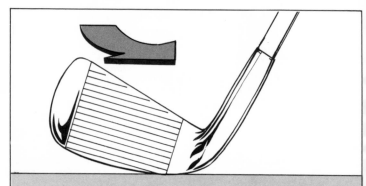

Fig 1.5. When the lie is too upright, the toe sits too far off the ground and promotes a pull or hook shot.

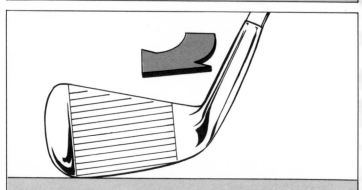

Fig 1.6. When the lie is too flat, the heel sits too far off the ground, and promotes a push or slice shot.

Which number clubs to buy

If you buy a set of clubs, this can consist of 9 or 10 irons, and 3 or 4 woods, plus a putter. Most off-the-shelf sets consist of 3 irons, sand iron, driver 3, and 5 wood. Very often you will have to buy the complete set of irons, but may not have to buy all three woods. In which case I recommend the clubs you should carry are 4 iron to sand wedge (leave the 3 iron indoors) and a 3 and 5 wood. My reasoning for this choice is based on the fact that the less lofted clubs, such as the 3 iron and driver, are more difficult to hit well. Their lack of loft means that the ball is contacted near its equator and thus more sidespin is imparted (Fig 1.7). This means that a slice or

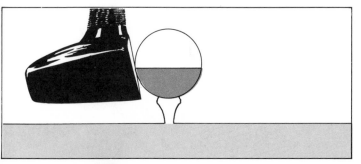

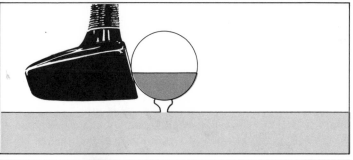

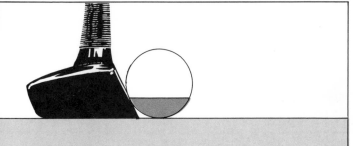

Fig 1.7. The straight-faced driver contacts the ball near its equator, imparting maximum sidespin. The more lofted clubs contact the ball lower down, thereby imparting more backspin and resulting in straighter shots.

hook is accentuated. The 3 wood has more loft than the driver, and will enable you quite adequately to hit the ball far enough off the tee. Likewise, a 3 iron has little loft, and unless you can hit yours consistently well, I recommend that you either leave it out of the bag, or include it only in case you need to hit a low shot under a tree. You would be better served by using the 5 wood, and women especially would benefit from using a 7 wood (roughly equivalent to a 3 or 4 iron) which many companies now make. Each of these lofted woods is also so useful out of the rough when distance is needed.

If you do insist on buying or using a driver, be sure that it has at least 12 degrees of loft – anything less will be very difficult to hit consistently well.

Ideally all players who are endeavouring to break 90, should steer away from the less lofted clubs, settle for more consistent accuracy, and do not be fooled into thinking that you *have* to hit a driver off every tee because your friends do. If their ability enables them to use this club consistently, then that is fine, but if you analyse their round, you may well find that their driver gets them into trouble too often. It is better to sacrifice 10 or 15 yards in distance, in order to be consistently on the fairway.

When choosing a putter, I would also recommend a heel and toe weighted model, which, like the irons and woods, will have a bigger sweet spot. Again there are many to choose from, so pick one that lies with its base on the ground, and that is the correct length for you.

The ball to use

If your goal is to break 90, do help yourself by playing with a decent golf ball. By that I mean one that is round, and without cuts or other serious imperfections, although slight paint grazes should not make too much difference. I would also recommend that you play the 'two-piece' golf ball, which has a solid core, is covered with a very resilient material, and whose structure promotes distance. Most manufacturers make this type of ball, which has a livelier feel to it than the alternative wound ball. For the higher-handicap player generally the extra control of the wound ball around the greens is worth sacrificing for the extra distance of the solid ball. However, for those who do prefer the wound ball, steer away from a Balata cover, which, since it is softer than the alternative Surlyn, promotes spin. Whilst this is fine for the better players who use this property to their advantage, it will exaggerate unwanted sidespin, making the ball slice or hook even more.

Summary

The above advice is not offered to make you dash to the professional's shop to spend money, but to make sure that you choose wisely. You may already have a good set of clubs, consisting of what I recommend, but I know from experience that once you have been 'bitten' by the game, you may wish to upgrade your equipment. The above advice will help, but always consult your professional, who will be only too willing to help you. The most expensive set of clubs will not turn a bad player into a good one, but if you have reached the standard of nearly breaking 90, then the correct equipment will start to make some difference to your play. Look after your clubs by keeping the grooves and grips clean, and at least then you will know that your clubs are not hindering you, but helping you to break 90.

CHAPTER TWO

Help for those who slice or hook

If you cannot quite break 90, the chances are that you either slice or hook the ball too often. Whilst this book does not set out to deal with badly struck shots in great detail, I want to give you some tips on how to minimize these faults, and learn how to live with them.

Help for those who slice

A slice is caused because the club face is aimed to the right of the swing path at impact, which imparts left-to-right sidespin on the ball (Fig 2.1). The reason for this is that the correct hand and forearm action through the impact zone is a far from natural movement for beginners, whose grip is seldom correct, and whose swing is often rather stiff and wooden. Their action fails to square the club face, leaving it open and creating left-to-right sidespin on the shot. To offset the ball veering to the right, the player then aims to the left, and in effect causes more sidespin by cutting even further across the ball. The sliced shot will go higher and travel less distance than it should for the club being used.

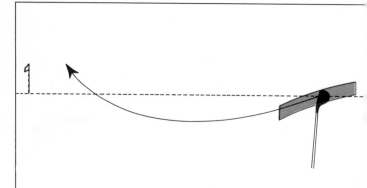

Fig 2.1. A sliced shot is caused by the club head travelling from out-to-in, with the club face aimed to the right of this path.

The grip

With the correct left-hand grip, where the club lies diagonally across the palm and fingers of the left hand (Fig 2.2), if you hold the club up in front of you, two-and-a-half to three knuckles should be visible (Fig 2.3). The 'V' formed by the thumb and forefinger should point to the right side of your face. When the right hand is placed on the grip, the 'V' formed should be parallel to that of the left, and pointing in the region of the right shoulder (Fig 2.4). Do not grip too tightly. The last three fingers of the left hand, and middle two of the right, should provide most of the pressure, which on a scale of one to five, with one being light and five being tight, should be about three to three-and-a-half. When you take your grip ensure that the club face is square to the target.

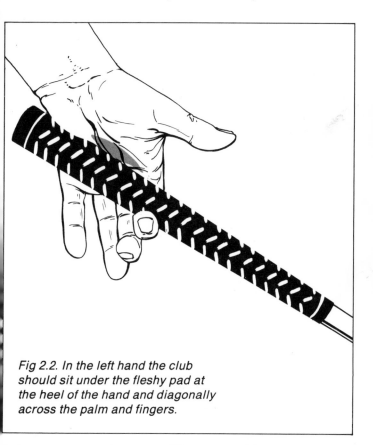

Fig 2.2. In the left hand the club should sit under the fleshy pad at the heel of the hand and diagonally across the palm and fingers.

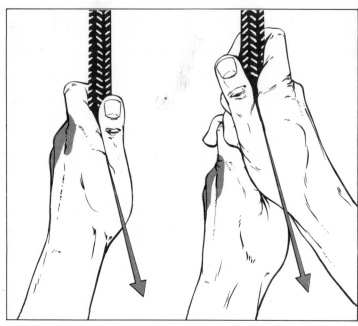

Fig 2.3. Those who slice should see 2½-3 knuckles of the left hand, and the 'V' of the thumb and forefinger should point to the right side of the face.

Fig 2.4. On the right hand the 'V' will point in the region of the right shoulder.

The set up

Most players who slice, have the ball too far forward in their stance, which pulls the shoulder line open (Fig 2.5). For your iron shots, the ball should be about three to four inches inside your left heel; for the fairway woods, about two to three inches inside the left heel; and for the driver and 3 wood, about one to two inches inside the left heel (Fig 2.6). With the ball more central you should now be able to take your address position with your shoulders parallel to the target line (Fig 2.7). Your left arm should be comfortably straight, but the right should be slightly softened at the elbow. Your feet, knees and hips must also be parallel to the target line. Your posture is also important, which means that you should bend forward from the hip bones, allowing your seat to stick out behind you as a counter-balance. The weight should be more

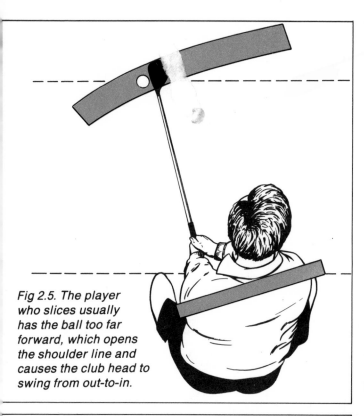

Fig 2.5. The player who slices usually has the ball too far forward, which opens the shoulder line and causes the club head to swing from out-to-in.

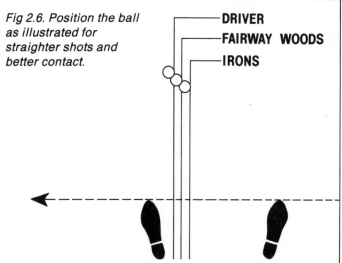

Fig 2.6. Position the ball as illustrated for straighter shots and better contact.

DRIVER
FAIRWAY WOODS
IRONS

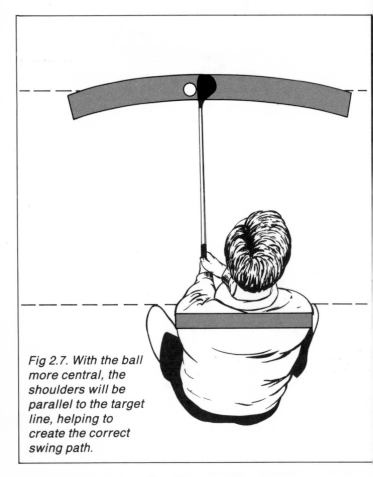

Fig 2.7. With the ball more central, the shoulders will be parallel to the target line, helping to create the correct swing path.

towards the ball of each foot, with the knees just flexed (Fig 2.8). Keep your chin up off your chest, and feel that your eyes are looking down at the ball.

The swing

This grip and set up will allow you to swing the club correctly to the inside of the target line during the backswing. Keep the club head fairly low to the ground for the first foot, which will encourage the body to turn, so that at the completion of the backswing your shoulders have turned 90 degrees. To help to this end, make certain that the right hip moves backwards, not laterally sideways (Fig 2.9a). You must allow your arms and

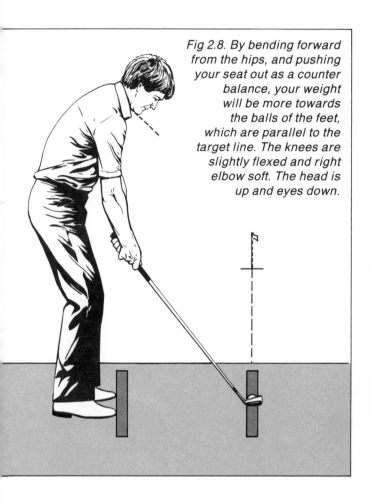

Fig 2.8. By bending forward from the hips, and pushing your seat out as a counter balance, your weight will be more towards the balls of the feet, which are parallel to the target line. The knees are slightly flexed and right elbow soft. The head is up and eyes down.

hands to dominate the downswing. Change direction by gently pulling down with the left arm, then allow both hands to strike the ball.

For the player who has sliced for some time, the wrists and hands will have to play a greater part in the swing, where the right hand and forearm will start to turn over the left just after impact (Fig 2.9b). Swing through the ball, not at it, so that you finish with your body facing the target, and the weight mainly on the outside of your left foot. To understand a little more how the hands and arms should work through the impact zone, stand with the club held horizontally in front of you, as if the ball was on a very high tee peg. Now swing to the right, then the left, and you will notice that just after the

Fig 2.9a. Turn the right hip backwards, not sideways, to create space in which the arms can swing.

Fig 2.9b. Allow the right hand and forearm to begin to rotate over the left just after impact.

a

b

club head passes your face, the right hand and forearm start to turn over the left (Fig 2.10). This action, which resembles a baseball swing, is similar to that in the correct golf swing.

Help for those who hook

The hooked shot is caused by the club face being closed, i.e. aimed to the left of the swing path at impact (Fig 2.11). This imparts right-to-left sidespin on the ball, causing it to curve in

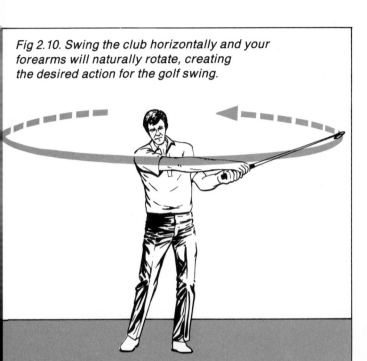

Fig 2.10. Swing the club horizontally and your forearms will naturally rotate, creating the desired action for the golf swing.

that direction. It also deducts loft from the club face, so that the ball flies lower than normal for the club being used. Since the ball finishes left of target, the player tends to aim to the right to allow for it, but this encourages an exaggerated inside attack on the ball, creating more hook spin (Fig 2.12). Players who are plagued by this type of shot are really not that far

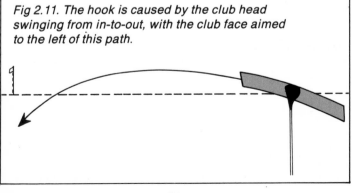

Fig 2.11. The hook is caused by the club head swinging from in-to-out, with the club face aimed to the left of this path.

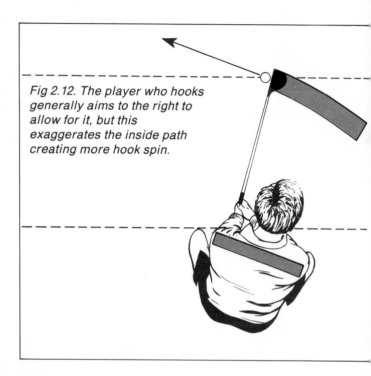

Fig 2.12. The player who hooks generally aims to the right to allow for it, but this exaggerates the inside path creating more hook spin.

from hitting the ball very well. They at least are able to attack the ball from inside the target line, and may well find that most of their problems are caused by a poor grip, and lack of good leg action.

The grip

Check that the two 'V's formed by the thumb and forefinger are not pointing too much to the right – ideally they should point slightly less to the right than recommended for the player who slices. Because you have good hand action, you should be able to see only two knuckles on the left hand rather than two-and-a-half to three (Fig 2.13).

The set up

Check that the ball is not played too far back in your stance, as this will tend to close the shoulder line. The ball should be positioned as explained in the slice section. The same goes for the rest of the set up (refer back to 'Help for those who slice')

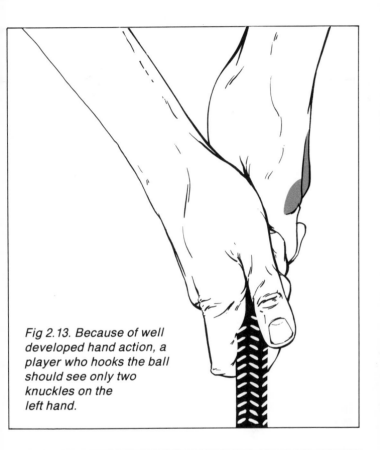

Fig 2.13. Because of well
developed hand action, a
player who hooks the ball
should see only two
knuckles on the
left hand.

The swing

When you swing the club, concentrate on keeping your arms
and body swinging in unison. The golfer who hooks violently,
often stops the body turning through the ball, which prevents
a good arm swing and forces the right hand to cross over the
left too abruptly (Fig 2.14). Try to swing to a balanced finish
so that through the impact zone, your right knee works
towards your left, with the right heel releasing from the
ground. This keeps your body turning and enables your arms
to continue swinging through the ball. Finish with your body
facing the target, and your weight on the outside of the left
foot (Fig 2.15). Concentrate on *pulling* the club head back to
the ball, feeling that the heel of the left hand leads. Never try
to hit the ball too hard, as this will emphasize the closing club
face. Take enough club, and swing smoothly.

Fig 2.14. When the body and legs fail to move through impact, they cause the hands and arms to rotate too suddenly and violently, closing the club face.

A set routine

Whether you slice or hook, you must always make allowances. The information above is designed to help you hit the ball with less sidespin, be that hook or slice. I have tried to help you *improve* the bad shot, but inevitably you will still spin the ball on many shots. However, I hope that your shots progress from slice and hook to fade and draw, each of these being a diluted form of sidespin shot. Whatever shaped shot you hit, the best way to cope is to allow for the curve. If you regularly hit the ball so that it curves 10 yards right to left, there is no use aiming at the pin only to see the ball finish 10

Fig 2.15. By finishing facing the target, with most of the weight on the outside of the left foot, your legs and body will be more likely to move correctly through impact, and enable you to keep the club face square.

yards to the left. Better to aim off where possible, so that the ball finishes on target.

The best way to go about this is to have a set routine, which will ensure that you set up to the ball as well as any professional. This is the stationary part of the game, so there is no reason why you cannot improve this aspect quite easily. Approach your routine as follows (Fig 2.16):

1 Stand facing the target and imagine the flight of your ball, so that it lands on target.

2 Pick out an intermediate target about three feet ahead of the ball on the line of flight.

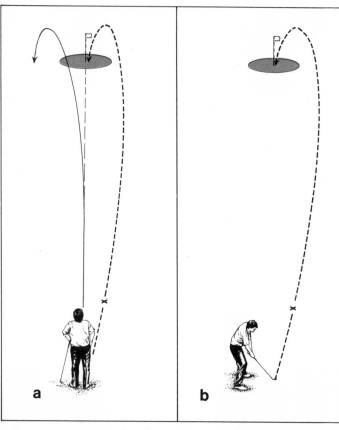

Fig 2.16a. If the ball generally curves to the left, do not aim at the target, because the ball will finish off-line. Use a routine where you stand behind the ball, visualize its flight, and then pick out an intermediate target just ahead of the ball on a line that allows for the curve.

Fig 2.16b. Aim the club face in line with this target and yourself parallel to the new target line.

3 Set up, ensuring that the club face is correctly aligned and that you are standing parallel to the initial line of flight. Remember that to break 90, you do not have to hit every shot straight. Try to decrease the amount of curve on your shots, and aim off to allow for this. Fairways and greens are not so narrow that only a straight shot will find them – you have some leeway, so do not despair.

CHAPTER THREE

Help for the ragged shots

You may not only hit shots that hook and/or slice, but also too many that are either topped or hit fat, or lack direction and distance. Golf is a demanding game, and having swung the club head about 20 feet through the air before impact, if it is as little as a quarter of an inch or a couple of degrees out of position, the shot is less than perfect, and often most disappointing (Fig 3.1).

There are a few points worth remembering about the golf swing that will help you break 90:

1 Under pressure, players tend to tighten their grip too much, and to swing too quickly. So take a firm but not vice-like grip, and try to keep the pressure constant throughout.

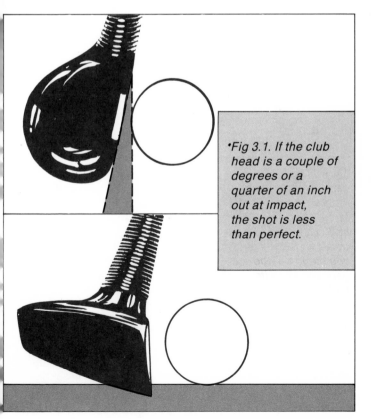

•Fig 3.1. If the club head is a couple of degrees or a quarter of an inch out at impact, the shot is less than perfect.

Fig 3.2. If the original spinal angle set at address rises, naturally the head must also be raised. Usually the ball is topped, or sometimes missed completely.

2 Use your practice swing to set the pace of swing for the shot, always being aware that you will tend to get faster as the pressure builds.

3 The rhythm of the swing is so important, but easily neglected. How often have you decided to play short of a hazard, taken an easy swing, and hit the ball so well that it is in danger of going into the hazard? That has happened to us all, and is a great lesson for demonstrating that when you swing smoothly, and in an unhurried manner, you strike the ball better, and it consequently goes further.

4 How many times has someone told you that you lifted your head when you hit a bad shot? Although this may be well-intentioned advice, it is seldom wholly correct. In an effort to hit the ball hard, the higher-handicap player will tend to use the body too much through the impact zone. This results in the original spinal angle set at address being raised, causing the ball to be topped (Fig 3.2). Naturally your head came up because your body came up. So try to keep the original spinal angle constant until the ball is struck. Swing your arms and hands, and let your body respond to that action. Certainly keep your head steady, trying to maintain its original height set at address, until you have struck the ball. Look at the ground long enough to see the tee peg or divot taken, but then allow your head to rotate towards the target. Trying to keep your head absolutely still is usually counter-productive, resulting in a very restricted action.

5 Do not rush the shots. So often if they are playing badly, golfers will rush to hit the next shot, not giving themselves a decent amount of time to aim and address the ball. The best professionals in the world would not play well if they did not take care at address. By all means walk quickly between shots, but take your time when you reach the ball. A few extra seconds on each shot will probably result in you hitting the ball less often, so the time taken to play the round will, in fact, be reduced.

CHAPTER FOUR

A better short game lowers scores

There is no question that the short game is the easiest part of your game to improve. It does not require a large open space in which to practise, nor does it need great strength. If you have a garden or can find a small area in which to work on this aspect of your game, then I assure you that your handicap and scores will come tumbling down. By spending even five minutes whenever possible, you can improve your action, and start to lower your score consistently.

I want to give you a few good tips on your technique. The following advice is for all short shots, excluding putting:

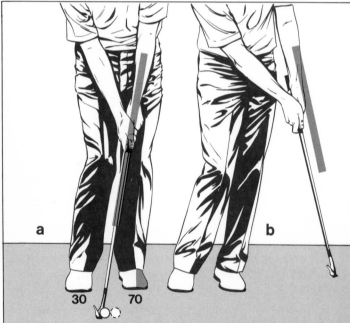

Fig 4.1a. For chips and pitches set up with a narrow open stance, the weight favouring the left side, and the left arm and shaft forming a straight line. This sets the hands ahead of the ball and club face. Play the ball inside the right foot for chips, and the left foot for pitches.
Fig 4.1b. Keep back of left wrist firm throughout stroke.

Fig 4.2. For pitches, swing
the club up steeply, keeping
the hands leading the
club head through impact.

Keep more weight on the left foot than the right. With your
stance narrow and open, but shoulders square to the target
line, place your weight more towards the outside of the left
foot, so that it favours that side in a ratio of about 70/30 or
60/40 (Fig 4.1a).

Position the ball just inside the *right* foot for chip shots,
and inside the *left* foot for pitches (Fig 4.1a).

Keep your hands ahead of the ball, so that the shaft slopes
towards the target. The left arm and shaft should form a
straight line (Fig 4.1a).

Use a firm-wristed action for all chip shots, keeping the
back of the left wrist in its address position throughout (Fig
4.1b).

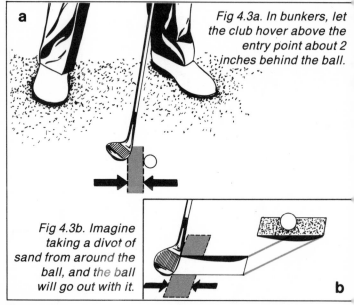

Fig 4.3a. In bunkers, let the club hover above the entry point about 2 inches behind the ball.

Fig 4.3b. Imagine taking a divot of sand from around the ball, and the ball will go out with it.

5 Try to swing the club back and through the same length.

6 For pitch shots swing the club back more steeply, but keep the hands leading the club face back into the ball (Fig 4.2).

7 *Never* try to hit the ball up into the air, or think of trying to *lift* it. Allow the club to descend slightly for chip shots, and more steeply for pitches, allowing the loft on the club to get the ball airborne.

8 For chips and pitches, feel that you are *pulling* the club head back into the ball, not *throwing* it at the ball.

9 Keep looking at the ground until the ball is well on its way.

10 In bunkers align your shoulders left of the target, be sure to swing back far enough, and endeavour to swing through the sand. Finish with your weight on the left foot, body facing the target, just as if it was a full swing.

11 For most bunker shots try to hit about two inches behind the ball, and let the club hover above that point at address, not at the back of the ball (Fig 4.3a).

12 Imagine taking a divot of sand from around the ball, and the ball will go out with it (Fig 4.3b).

13 Keep the swing long and smooth, rather than making it short and stabbing.

Putting

1 Use a firm-wristed action, where the angles at the back of each wrist remain constant (Fig 4.4).

2 Accelerate the putter through the ball.

3 Keep the body and head still. To prevent looking up too quickly, try to guess where the ball has gone. You may guess wrong, but your putting should improve.

4 To encourage a smooth action, try to keep the putter blade in contact with the ball for as long as possible.

All of the above points will improve your golf. You must be honest with yourself, and try to assess which points are missing from your game, then gradually incorporate them one or two at a time. If, for example, your chipping always lets you down, just check the points above and you may solve your problem. Do not expect to remember everything in one go. Take one or two points, and make a determined effort to work on them during your next round or practice session.

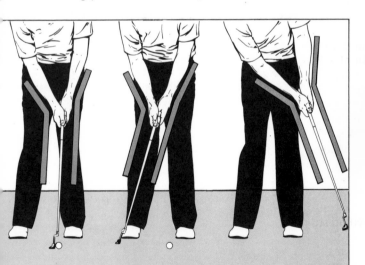

Fig 4.4. Use a firm-wristed putting stroke where the angles at the back of the wrists remain constant.

CHAPTER FIVE

Golf – the outdoor game of chess

The art of low scoring involves good planning as well as good striking. I do believe that it is as much a case of discipline as talent to get the best from yourself. Whilst we have all seen top-class professional playing, few of us are witness to their thoughts or plans on how to play the course. What I can tell you is that they put a lot of thought not only into each shot, but on how to play each hole. Regardless of the fact that they are quite capable of hitting their driver straight a high percentage of times, they will not pull that club from the bag at every par 4 or 5. They, and their caddy, will have worked out the best plan for getting the ball round the course in the lowest number of shots. Players of this calibre know that ego must give way to common sense, and striking the ball 250 yards with the driver may not put them into the best position for the second shot. Naturally their ability allows them to perform to a high standard quite easily and regularly, but you must adopt the same procedure, and put as much mental effort into the game as they do.

We cannot see their minds working, but I can assure you that the top players' minds are far more active and take in many more factors than those of any middle to high-handicap amateurs. So before you venture onto the course, here are a few words of advice about your pre-round preparation.

Warm up first

Try to arrive in time to warm up. Ideally you should hit some shots, but more realistically most people either do not have the time or the facilities do not permit this. Even before you swing a club it would be helpful to stretch your muscles, by just turning your upper body to the right then left, and gently swinging your arms in circles to either side of your body. The last thing you want to do is pull a muscle. Next swing a club, starting with a short iron and then working up to a wood. Some people benefit from swinging two clubs at once, the extra weight gently helping to stretch the muscles. If possible chip a few shots, and have several putts, all of which will serve to give you an idea of the pace of the greens. Get your score card, tee pegs, ball, towel and markers organized so that you can go to the first tee knowing that you have prepared yourself and can concentrate calmly on the shot in hand.

Practise your hitting

At this stage of your progress you should also know how far you expect to hit each club. It would be well worthwhile spending some time on the practice ground in order to find out. Take about 20 balls, all similar to the ones you use. For instance, if you use a solid two-piece ball, and I recommend that you do, try to use 20 solid balls, not those of driving-range quality, or a wound ball. Try to pick a calm day, perhaps in the spring or autumn (fall) when the ground is not rock hard. Obviously the ball will run when it lands, but better to underestimate the total length of the shot than get flattering results during a long dry summer.

From a level, and good lie, hit your shots starting perhaps with a 9 iron. Do not try to hit the shots flat out, but at the pace and strength you would normally use. Then pace out to the centre of where the majority of the balls have landed. Ignore those you may have mis-hit and the one or two that have gone further than the rest. You want a good average yardage. Most people can readily pace a yard, but it would be worth checking your stride length.

If you continue this process for all the odd numbered clubs, you will then be able to gauge the even numbers from them. Depending on your strength, you may have a difference of about 10–15 yards per club. How far you hit each club is not that important, but being able to judge distances on the course and translating that into club choice is important. There is no point in hitting your 7 iron, say, 135 yards one minute, then 150 the next – correct clubbing will become impossible. This is why the professionals know the distance to the pin and are able to hit a ball yard perfect so often; good rhythm and striking enables them to hit the correct depth of shot time and time again.

If you are not able to go through this procedure, make use of the yardage at the short holes on your course. On a calm day, note which club hits the ball to the middle of the green, and use that as a guide. Some courses have markers at certain points on the course, say, 150 yards, to indicate distance, and many now have yardage charts, which may prove useful. If your course has neither, keep a note of which clubs you use from certain points (do this on a calm day), or make your own yardage chart of the course.

CHAPTER SIX

Planning your round

Most courses have a par value of between 68 and 72, with ladies' courses being perhaps one or two shots more. For the sake of practicality, I want to assume that par is 70, so that if you drop a shot a hole, you will break 90. In other words, playing to a handicap of 18 is a comparative standard to breaking 90. This means that the par values of each hole on the course must now be assessed differently, with the 3s becoming par 4s, 4s now 5s, and 5s now 6s. If you view the course in this manner, you will take pressure off yourself, and you can plan each hole more realistically (Fig 6.1).

Par 3s

Let us first look closely at how best to play a par 3 hole. Since these vary so much in length, you must first assess whether you can in fact reach the green. Whilst very few men have trouble with distance on a par 3, many ladies may be better of laying up short of the hole on the longer par 3s, especially

Fig 6.1. Mentally change the par values of each hole in order to take pressure off yourself.

COMPETITION .... DATE ....
PLAYER A... PLAYER B ....
HANDICAP........... STROKES REC'D........... HANDICAP........... STROKES REC'D...........

Marker's Score	Hole	Yards	Metres	Par	Yards	Metres	Stroke index	Players Score A	B	Won + Lost − Halved o
	1	423	387	A5	417	382	7			
	2	176	161	34	160	146	13			
	3	389	355	A5	382	349	3			
	4	380	348	A5	354	324	9			
	5	147	135	34	132	121	15			
	6	335	307	A5	326	298	17			
	7	392	358	A5	381	349	5			
	8	422	386	A5	407	372	1			
	9	505	462	36	498	455	11			
OUT		3169	2899	35 44	3057	2796				

36

Fig 6.2. On a par 3, the shorter hitter may be wise to lay up in a safe area short of the green.

SAFE LAY-UP
AREA

where there are cavernous bunkers placed to catch the short shot (Fig 6.2). If the last few times you have played a hole, you have landed in the front bunkers, then either take one or two more clubs, or decide to play short. I said earlier that golf required discipline, and it is not easy to make yourself play short of the green on a par 3, but ladies, where there is a grassy area for you to lay up, do that rather than plug the ball in the bunker. Most middle to high-handicap players would rather hit from grass than sand, so bear that in mind.

Do not think that I am going to turn you into a purely defensive golfer — I'm not. However, I want you to become an honest and thinking type of player. According to our earlier plan, this par 3 is now a par 4, so you can still be on the green in two, putting for a three, but with a greater chance of making four. Par 3s well within range, provide a golden opportunity to 'pick up' a shot if you can hit the green. You must first consider which club to use based on the tee and pin positions, the weather and your knowledge, perhaps newly found, of how far you hit each club. As a general rule, you should be aiming to hit the middle of every green, but on very long greens, if the pin is at the back, you will need a longer club. If the pin is at the front, it may not be prudent to take a shorter iron if it means that a slightly mis-hit shot may land in a bunker (Fig 6.3).

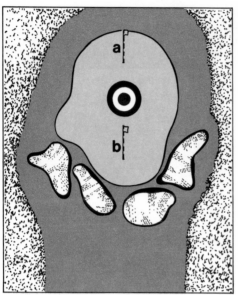

Fig 6.3.
Generally you should aim to hit the middle of each green, but if the pin is at the back, take a longer club. If the pin is at the front, remember that if you mis-hit a shorter club, the ball could land in the bunker.

If a hole is downwind, you may need one or two clubs less, depending on the wind strength. Into the wind always take more club than for the yardage, rather than trying to hit the ball harder, which only spins the ball faster, sending it higher into the air. Take one or two clubs more, perhaps grip down, and swing smoothly. Cross winds will obviously affect the ball, and may require you to take a longer club when the wind is strong. Always put the ball on a tee peg, which will give you the best opportunity of a clean strike. Take note if the greenkeeper has moved the tee boxes any considerable amount forward or back of the fixed yardage marker, since four or five yards difference here may just swing the balance of club choice.

One more point to remember about all tee shots, and that is not to be influenced by the direction in which the tee points, because it does *not* always aim directly at the green or down the fairway. By picking the intermediate target just ahead of the ball you should be able to disregard where the tee aims.

Par 4s

Your par 4 strategy needs more study. Under the plan of now playing it as if it was a par 5, you are allowed three shots to reach the green. On some holes this may be needed, but on

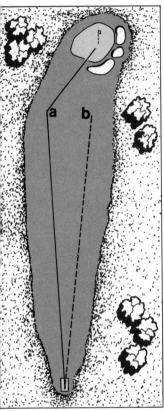

Fig 6.4. If you can see the pin
position, aim your tee
shot to give yourself an
easier second shot
avoiding the hazards.

others the green will be in
range, provided that you put
your tee shot into play. As you
survey the hole, decide, being
realistic, from where you wish
to play your second shot, and
indeed your third. You should
base your plan on the layout of
the hole, and even the pin
position, provided that you can
see the green. For instance, if the hole is a fairly short par 4,
with no severe bunkers in play from the tee, if the pin is cut on
the right side of the green behind a bunker, you would have a
better approach from the left side of the fairway (Fig 6.4).

I realise that you may not have the ability to always hit the
ball off the tee exactly where you wish, but where
circumstances allow, consider from which side of the fairway
it is better to approach. However, the one vital rule to follow
is to avoid bunkers off the tee. If the fairway narrows down
just where your tee shot lands, and there are bunkers either
side, do consider playing a club that positions the ball short of
these hazards (Fig 6.5). It is usually very difficult to gain
much distance from a bunker, and you are putting yourself
under extra pressure by subsequently having a longer third
shot to the green. This is where your on-course discipline
must prevail. If all your playing partners take their drivers and
successfully hit the fairway, you may feel under pressure to
follow suit. Keep to your game plan and you will prove to

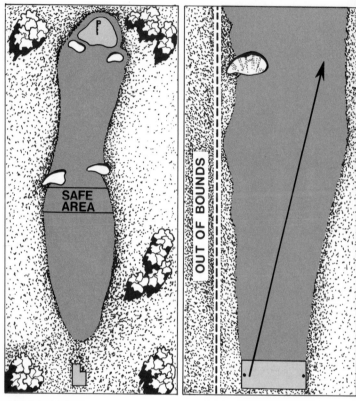

Fig 6.5. If there are bunkers in the landing area, lay up short of them.

Fig 6.6. Provided that you hit the ball fairly straight, tee upon the same side as any trouble, which will encourage you to aim away from it.

yourself that you can score better by playing sensibly.

When teeing the ball, the general rule is to tee up on the same side of the tee as the trouble (Fig 6.6). In other words, if there is a bunker or out of bounds on the left side of the fairway, to help you to aim away from them, play from the left side of the tee. Whereas this advice works well on open courses and for the player who hits the ball reasonably straight, if your shots curve quite a lot, then you cannot follow this advice totally. If you play on a tight tree-lined course and your shots start left and then slice, by teeing up on the left

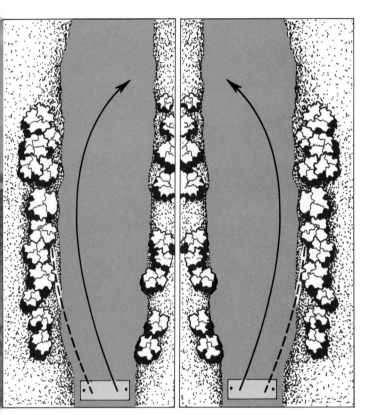

Fig 6.7. If your shots start left and then fade, on a tree-lined hole you need to tee up on the right side of the tee, or otherwise the ball will hit the trees.

Fig 6.8. If your shots start right and then draw, on a tree-lined hole you need to tee up on the left side of the tee, or otherwise the ball will hit the trees.

side you are more likely to hit the trees on that side (Fig 6.7). You must favour the right side of the tee, and allow your slice or fade to curve the ball away from the trouble. Of course, the opposite applies for players whose shots start right, then draw or hook. They should play from the left side of the tee, giving themselves room to aim well wide of trouble up the left, and to avoid the trees down the right side (Fig 6.8).

When playing dog-leg holes take care not to 'bite off' too much of the angle and land in trouble. Whilst taking the brave line on these holes may appear more spectacular, it is always

41

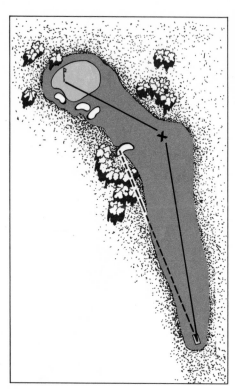

Fig 6.9. Avoid cutting
off too much of the
dog leg, or the ball
will land in trouble,
or leave you a more
difficult second shot.

a higher risk shot, so bear that in mind (Fig 6.9).

Once your tee shot is in play, your next decision is whether you can easily reach the green. If you need to hit your longest club very well to reach it, you should think carefully if this is the right choice. Are there bunkers short of the green to catch a slightly mis-hit shot, or are there no intervening hazards between you and the hole? If there are bunkers, I would suggest that you lay up short of them, then pitch on (Fig 6.10). Remember this par 4 is a par 5 in our plan. If you can reach the green easily, consider your club selection based on the same facts as described for the par 3 hole.

Do not blindly be drawn into aiming at the pin every time, because if it is cut to one side of the green close to a bunker or water, there is a risk that a slightly mis-hit shot will land in this trouble (Fig 6.11). If you can get the ball onto the centre portion of the green you will never be too far from the pin. More golfers under-club than over-club and, generally speaking, most trouble is at the front of the greens, so make a promise to yourself to take enough club.

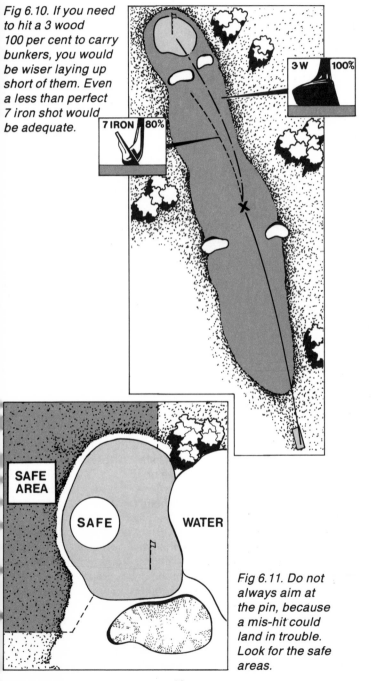

Fig 6.10. If you need to hit a 3 wood 100 per cent to carry bunkers, you would be wiser laying up short of them. Even a less than perfect 7 iron shot would be adequate.

3 W 100%

7 IRON 80%

SAFE AREA

SAFE

WATER

Fig 6.11. Do not always aim at the pin, because a mis-hit could land in trouble. Look for the safe areas.

43

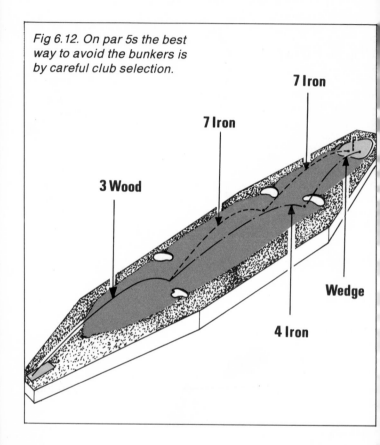

Fig 6.12. On par 5s the best way to avoid the bunkers is by careful club selection.

Par 5s

Certainly for the longer hitters, these holes present a golden opportunity to pick up a shot. Our plan says that they are par 6s, but the longer hitter will have no trouble lengthwise in reaching the green in three shots, probably making a true par 5, and even a true birdie, a possibility. So let us examine how the longer hitter should approach this type of hole. Whilst I know that it does depend on the exact length of the hole, it is feasible that you could reach the green using a 3 wood, and then, say, two 6 iron shots. So do not be tempted to stand on the tee and thrash at the ball. Using the same principles as for the tee shot on the par 4, select your club and carefully aim the shot. Before you hit your second shot, consider the task and hazards before you. Very often on par 5s there is a second set of bunkers short of the green, and you definitely want to avoid them (Fig 6.12). This is where the discipline of playing an iron, rather than a fairway wood, may be needed. Again, depending on your strength, select the club that will safely land the ball short of the trouble. You could play perhaps a 6 or 7 iron, leaving yourself a slightly longer shot to the green, or play a 4 iron, leaving only a short pitch shot (Fig 6.12). The choice is yours, and your ability at playing each of these shots must dictate and influence your choice. There is no one right way. You may love hitting your 7 iron, and hate the 4, in which case the former option would suit you better. If the lie of the ball is good, and you feel that you can easily carry the bunkers, then play that shot, and you will hopefully set up a birdie chance by leaving yourself only a short pitch to the green. For the longer hitter the most annoying thing is to take four shots to reach the green, so use your head, avoid trouble, and you should be putting for a gross birdie!

The shorter-hitting player has to plan to be on the green in four shots, which should not be too difficult. The chances are that the fairway bunkers will not be in range from the tee, and if there are further bunkers, say, 80–100 yards short of the green, you want to be short of them in three shots. Your lack of length in some ways makes planning easier because you are less tempted to try to carry distant hazards, and tee shots are less likely to reach the first set. By planning thus, you too should be on the green in four, in theory putting for a true par, so approach par 5 holes with pleasure and eagerness.

Perhaps a sobering thought for the more aggressive and less reliable player, is that most men could hit three 5 iron shots about 480 yards, enough distance to reach many par 5 holes!

Playing partners' influence

I wrote earlier that you must not be drawn into hitting your driver, just because your playing partners do. Always try to keep to your game plan for each hole, rather than being drawn into a long driving contest. But you can use your partners' play to good effect. If, for instance, you have all selected an iron to hit to a par 3, and all your partners' shots finish short, then maybe the wind strength or the actual distance have been misjudged. This is the time to consider whether to take a longer club. Of course it is possible that they all hit their shots very badly, but you may be able to learn from their mistakes.

CHAPTER SEVEN

To attack or defend?

The last chapter offered general advice on how to play different holes, but one of the most difficult choices on the course is knowing when to attack and when to defend. The fact that you are trying to break 90 means that it is a medal round, where you should err on the side of caution rather than reckless abandon. One high scoring hole in a match or stableford competition does not ruin the chance of winning, but a 9 or 10 in a medal round will undoubtedly make your original target much harder to achieve. But attack is not out of the question altogether; it is simply a matter of knowing where and when. The main points to consider are:

1 How the ball lies.
2 How you are playing on that particular day.
3 The outcome if the gamble fails.
4 Is the gamble necessary?

Apart from tee shots, the lie of the ball is purely a matter of luck. If you are wishing to hit a 3 wood from the fairway and the ball is in a divot or depression, then you have a problem, and hitting that club would not be wise (Fig 7.1). If, on the other hand, the ball is sitting up nicely in the rough, then you may even be able to use your 3 wood if a long shot is needed. So do not make up your mind about which club to hit until you have seen how the ball is sitting. If the ball is in the rough, the number-one rule is to get it back onto the fairway, using the club that has sufficient loft to make the shot possible. Do not try to carry a bunker perhaps 50 yards ahead

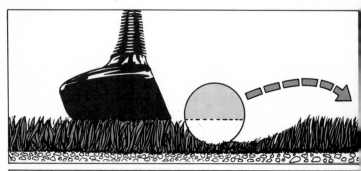

Fig 7.1. If the ball is lying in a divot or in a depression, then a 3 wood is not the club to use.

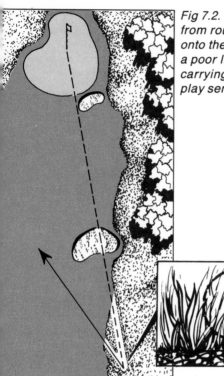

Fig 7.2. The number-one rule from rough, is to get back onto the fairway. From a poor lie do not risk carrying a bunker but play sensibly.

f the ball is nestled down, because there is every possibility that it will come out low and run into the bunker (Fig 7.2). Aim away from the bunker and just accept that an errant shot means you must lose some distance. Do not compound the error by trying to play an impossible shot and risk a high score. Do not rely on trying to shape a shot from the rough, because the intervening grass between the club face and ball prevents you from imparting the desired sidespin. For this reason, those of you whose natural shots curve considerably, may find that you hit the ball straighter from the light rough.

No matter how much you may practise, your standard of golf will fluctuate, and certain shots or clubs that presented no problem a week ago can suddenly become quite unreliable. You may suddenly find that you have topped your favourite 5 wood all day. It would therefore not be prudent to try to carry a distant ditch or bunker with that club, but accept that, for today anyway, you must change your plan and hit a 5 iron and then, say, a 9 iron. It is very difficult to put bad shots out of your mind, and, although I will deal with that subject later on, you should not put yourself under additional pressure by persisting in playing certain shots or clubs that are currently unsuccessful. Conversely, you may be having a day where you are playing much better than usual, in which case your quality of strike will allow you to be more attacking. But do not be lulled into thinking that anything is possible – try to maintain a realistic outlook and remember to adhere to your plan on how to play each hole.

Being realistic must be uppermost in your mind when you take any gamble on the golf course. It is not a negative attitude to consider what will happen if the gamble does not succeed – it will make you think better and help you to consider the perhaps less spectacular alternatives. It is probably not worth the risk of carrying a far-off ditch or bunker if you are not going to reach the green (Fig 7.3); better to lay up short and then pitch on. If the lie is good, and you have been playing your fairway woods very well, you may feel that it is worth the chance of being closer to the green, but this goes back to the previous points – that the lie of your ball and your play must both influence the choice of shot. If you were to go into the ditch, you would be penalized a shot, so think carefully before you play.

Despite the fact that you may not yet be a low-handicap player, there is no reason why you should not try on certain occasions to shape different shots. If your ball has landed behind some trees, you may decide to hook a shot round them. This is not a particularly risky shot in the right circumstances, but what would be the outcome should the ball either not curve enough or curve too violently (Fig 7.4). It may be wiser, though perhaps less exciting, to play a short

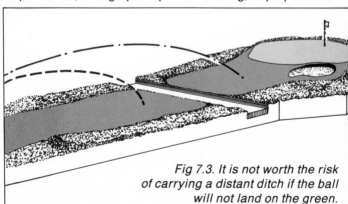

Fig 7.3. It is not worth the risk of carrying a distant ditch if the ball will not land on the green.

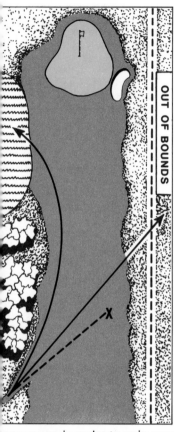

Fig 7.4. If you decide to curve a shot intentionally what will happen if the ball curves too much or not enough? Would it be wiser to play a less spectacular shot back onto the fairway?

OUT OF BOUNDS

shot to the middle of the fairway. If a shot is first of all considered a gamble, you must then ask yourself if the gamble is necessary or are you purely pandering to your ego. In many Pro-Ams I play, if one of my partners is in trouble I will point out their shot options. More often than not they will opt for the more spectacular, high-risk shot, which may involve threading the ball through quite a narrow gap in order to gain maybe a 30 yard advantage over the alternative choice. Whilst in a Pro-Am format, where it is a better-ball competition, this cavalier approach can be acceptable, I feel certain that most of these players would still go for the same shot in a medal round. This can be great fun, but not conducive to breaking 90 on a regular basis. Some people are gamblers by nature, and for them keeping their attacking spirit under control is paramount to consistency. Whilst they may excel in matchplay and stableford events, a medal round demands that they curb their gambling tendency until such time that better technique permits them to be more interested in breaking 80 than 90. If you keep to the par 4, 5 and 6 plan, you should start to produce better scores, and once you become more used to playing conservatively, it will not feel so restrictive. You must always guard against gambling just once too often, which could ruin your chance of a sub-90 round.

CHAPTER EIGHT

Short game strategy

I have already stated that one of the easiest ways to lower your score is to improve your short game, I have also advised you on how to play certain shots, but choosing the right shot to play is very important, too. The essential factor in the short game is being able to visualize the shot to play. If you have to play from 140 yards away, you will simply choose the club that hits the ball that distance. But when faced with a shot of say, 75 yards, then you have several alternatives from which to choose (Fig 8.1). So let us consider how you should approach any short game shot.

1 Check the lie of the ball. This will determine which shots may or may not be possible. If the ball is sitting in a depression, then to play a high floating shot is not possible. If the lie is good, then your choice of shot is not too limited.

2 Are there intervening hazards or rough ground between your ball and the hole? If there are, then the ball must travel mainly through the air. If there are not, the ground route is the easier option (Fig 8.2).

3 How will the shape and contours and speed of the fairway fringe and green affect the roll of the ball?

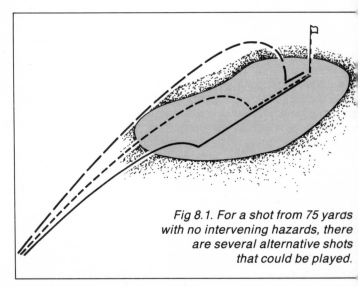

Fig 8.1. For a shot from 75 yards with no intervening hazards, there are several alternative shots that could be played.

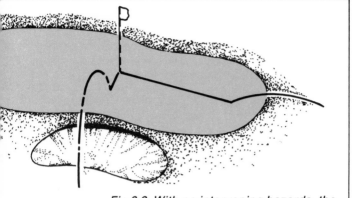

Fig 8.2. With no intervening hazards, the low running shot is the easier option, but the ball must take the air route when bunkers are on your line.

Ideally if you do not hole the chip or pitch shot, and let us be honest and admit that although this is possible, it is not probable, then where do you want the ball to finish? Uphill putts are easier than downhill or sidehill ones, so if possible try to leave the easy putt. If the green is flat, then be positive and get used to 'seeing' the ball finish past the hole.

These are the main factors to consider *before* you select the club. The lower-handicap player will automatically tend to go through this thought process, whilst the high scorers will not. I played a round of golf with a pupil of mine, whose swing was really very good, but whose handicap did not seem to reflect her skill. I asked her to talk me through her thoughts about each shot before she played it. On the long shots she quite correctly considered the hazards and areas to avoid, but on those from 100 yards in, she failed to consider enough about how the ball was going to react when it landed, and therefore often played the wrong choice of shot.

Shot options must be determined by these factors, but they must also be governed by which shot you feel happiest with and are most successful at playing. I have played with many ladies who are deadly at running the ball onto the green with their 7 iron from all sorts of places. This, I would find more difficult and would choose to play a wedge or sand wedge so that the ball is lofted onto the putting surface, which will eliminate the chances of it getting a bad kick on the fairway or fringe. For me, my choice of shot is more reliable, but that does not make me right and them wrong. Whilst in text book terms the ideal shot to play is usually the one that avoids possible deflections from the area in front of the green, this must be balanced by your ability to play certain shots. Having said all that, I would like to offer some advice on club choice, which should help to clarify matters for you.

Situation 1

The ball is 3 yards short of the green, which slopes from left to right, with the pin at the back, and no intervening hazards (Fig 8.3). If the fringe is smooth and even, the first and easiest option is to putt the ball. You will be consistently more successful with this club in this situation, than chipping the ball. You will also do less damage score-wise if you mis-hit it – a badly hit putt is better than a badly hit chip. If the ground is uneven, or the grass is long or wet, then the ball needs to be lofted onto the front edge of the green so that it can roll up to the pin. The club choice for this shot is one without too much loft. You could use any club between an 8 and 5 iron quite successfully. Remember, the lower the number the lower the ball will go, and the more it will roll. I personally rarely chip with a club less lofted than a 7 iron, mainly because I find that I have a better control of the ball this way. However you should select a club within this range. The wrong club to use would be one with a lot of loft, such as a wedge or sand wedge. You would need to hit it harder to cover the distance, so if it is mis-hit the consequences are more disastrous; it is also more difficult to judge how hard to hit the ball through the air than along the ground. Having selected your club, aim off to the left of the pin to allow for the ground to take the ball to the hole. If you find that your

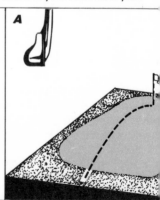

Fig 8.3. The ball is 3 yards off the green, which slopes from left to right:
A If the ground is smooth, the easiest option is to putt, aiming left of the pin.
B If the ground is uneven, chip and roll the ball with a club such as a 7 iron, aiming left of the pin.
C The hardest shot is a pitch or chip with a wedge.

chip shots are almost always short of the hole, try chipping a less lofted club, i.e., use a 7 instead of an 8, but hit the ball using the same strength. The straighter-faced club will help the ball to roll further.

Situation 2

The ball is 20 yards short of the green, with the pin cut near the back. The green slopes up towards the back, and the pin is cut close to the back left edge, where there is also a bunker (Fig 8.4). This shot could be played in several different ways, but you must consider what could happen if the shot goes wrong. If you choose to pitch the ball all the way to the hole, using, say, a wedge or sand wedge, but pulled the shot slightly, the ball could land in the bunker. If you hit the ball on line but too long, you could be off the green – the only thing that could prevent this is the fact that the green is uphill from front to back. So if you opt for the air route, do not be drawn into aiming at the pin, but aim instead at the heart of the green. This way the bunker presents no danger, and you will leave an uphill putt.

You could choose to play a lower shot with a less lofted club so that the ball will run up the slope. Use perhaps an 8 or 9 iron, and play the ball just back of centre, so that you get a slightly more penetrating shot than normal. There are no real problems with this shot option, but your main task is to judge how hard to hit the ball. The fact that an uphill putt is preferable may persuade you to err on the side of being short rather than long.

If you are proficient at judging how far to pitch the ball, then you should choose the first option, but if you have problems judging pitch shots then play the alternative.

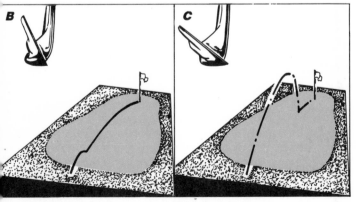

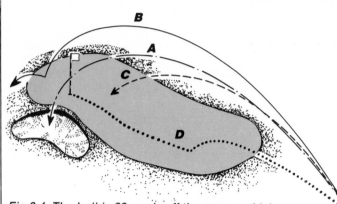

Fig 8.4. The ball is 20 yards off the green, which is slightly uphill, and the pin is cut near the back left edge:
A *Using a wedge, if you aim for the pin, a slightly mis-hit shot may find the bunker.*
B *If you hit the ball too far, it could go off the green into trouble, and you will have a downhill shot back.*
C *Play a wedge shot sensibly for the heart of the green, leaving an uphill putt.*
D *You may prefer to play a lower running shot with perhaps an 8 iron, which is an easier alternative than shot C for the higher-handicap golfer.*

Situation 3

The ball is 15 yards to the left of the green, but a bunker lies between it and the hole. The ball is sitting quite well, with a cushion of grass beneath it. On the other side of the green, directly beyond the hole, is another deep bunker (Fig 8.5). Since the ball is sitting well, the best club to use is your most lofted, i.e., the sand wedge. The good lie will allow the deep flange to slide beneath the ball, so that the shot in itself is not difficult to execute. What is more difficult is to judge how hard to hit the ball so that it carries the first bunker but does not run off the green into the second.

Depending on your ability with this club and type of shot, you must decide where to aim. The very last thing you want is for the ball to land in either bunker, so if you decide to aim at the pin, do not try to be too clever by hitting the ball so that it barely clears the first bunker. With this in mind, it is obviously all too easy to hit the ball too hard so that it rolls into the far

unker. So this is a high-risk option and, as a general guide, I
would suggest that by aiming slightly away from the pin you
will be playing an easier and less risky shot. You will still have
chance of single putting, and, more importantly, you will
have eliminated the possibility of dropping more shots than
necessary. To get the ball anywhere on the green is better
than putting it in a bunker. For those less confident with this
type of shot, there is nothing wrong with playing the ball,
even perhaps with a 7 iron, more towards the front of the
green, so that it does not even have to carry a bunker. From
here you can still two-putt and you will have avoided any
great disasters. You must not allow the pin to act like a

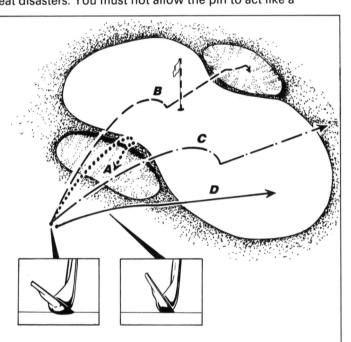

*Fig 8.5. The ball is off the green with a bunker between
it and the pin. It is sitting well, but the green
is narrow with a bunker on the far side:*
***A & B** Using a sand wedge and aiming at the pin, it is
easy to under- or over-hit the ball, so it lands in a bunker.*
***C** The safer shot is to use a sand wedge and play
away from the pin, so that if the ball is hit too
hard it will roll onto the fringe.*
***D** You could use a 7 iron and play towards
the front of the green rather than find a bunker.*

magnet, but instead allow your ability and discipline to be your guides.

If this situation occurred but the ball was lying badly, most players would be better playing towards the front of the green. The alternative could easily be to thin the ball into the face of the near bunker or a long way over the green.

The number of examples is endless, but I hope that these three serve to show the thought process necessary, whatever the options.

Bunkers

Ideally these should be avoided at all cost, but no matter how well you play, the ball will land in one at some time. Sadly, so many high-handicap players have poor bunker technique, so try to improve yours. The golden rule is to get out in one shot, ideally towards the hole, but if this is not possible, then either sideways or backwards will suffice. From a reasonable lie, where the bunker is not too deep, forwards should be possible, but in very deep bunkers, look to see if by playing sideways or backwards you stand a better chance of hitting your next shot from grass, rather than sand, which is what most golfers prefer. Again, do not let the pin distract or attract you too much; if you are not too good out of bunkers, settle for getting the ball on the green. I am always being asked how to play the ball when it has just rolled into the back of the bunker, settling onto a downhill lie, with a steep bunker face between it and the hole. The answer, if you cannot break 90, is that you do not play the shot. Even for the professional this is far from easy, so either play sideways or backwards.

Bunker shots of 30 yards and upwards are difficult, so guard against trying to hit the ball too hard and losing your footing. Consider what would be the worst shot that you could play, and then plan accordingly. Is the ball lying on top of or down in the sand? If you take too much sand will the ball land in another bunker just ahead? If you hit it a little thin and it goes too far, is there great danger over the green? How good are you at playing this particular shot? All these questions must be answered before the ball is played.

Similar questions should be considered before you play fairway bunker shots. If you decide to try for a long shot and it is not successful, will the ball go into another bunker or ditch, or just end up on the fairway short of the green. Try to assess the outcome, based on your ability, the lie of the ball, and the pressure you feel at the time.

CHAPTER NINE

Putting strategy

Many higher-handicap golfers neglect this department of the game. When you first decide on golf as a leisure activity, naturally your main task is to learn to hit the ball a decent distance and direction. This is quite acceptable and understandable, but once you have started to improve in that respect, you *must* look to your putting as one of the easiest routes to lower scoring. Most poor putters lack two things: a reliable putting stroke, and the ability to apply that stroke to its greatest effect.

Once your action is adequate, how can you use it to maximum benefit? Assessing a putt begins before you get to the green, because as you are walking along the fairway, you are better able to see if the whole green slopes in one particular direction or another. This is especially important when you play on hilly or undulating courses, where the true slope of the green can be difficult to judge. As a rule, the green will follow the slope of the surrounding land (Fig 9.1).

As you walk onto the green, look at the grass. Greens can vary from hole to hole, as well as from course to course, so try to assess if the green on which you are playing looks quicker or slower than the last green.

It is as important that you adopt a routine for your putting as your long game. Ideally if it is possible, and not too time

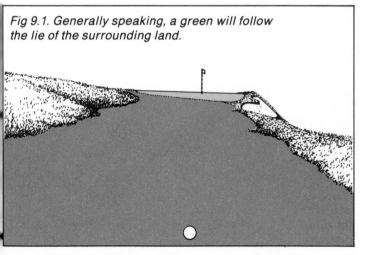

Fig 9.1. Generally speaking, a green will follow the lie of the surrounding land.

consuming, walk from the hole back to your ball. As you walk, look at the line of the putt for any pitch marks that you can repair, and remove any stones or other loose impediments on your line. Whilst walking you can *feel* through your feet and legs if there are any slopes or contours. On very long putts I like to stop halfway, and then view the putt from the side, at this point trying to visualize how fast the ball must start, in order to be *dying* at the hole. Then take a look at your putt from behind the ball, carefully noting the borrows within one yard to either side of the hole, since these will have the greatest effect on the ball as it travels slowly at this point. Once you have chosen the line, have a practice putt to familiarize yourself with the correct strength. Meanwhile, look along the line of the putt, visualizing the ball rolling and then dropping into the hole. Where possible, pick a spot about two feet ahead of the ball and use that as an intermediate target – just as you did with the long game.

It is unlikely at this stage that you have become so good that you are able to hit the ball exactly where you wish all the time. The professionals may be able to putt the ball quarter-inch perfect, and so it is worth them taking plenty of time on their putts. I want you to take enough time, but not to take up residence on the green! Provided that you give

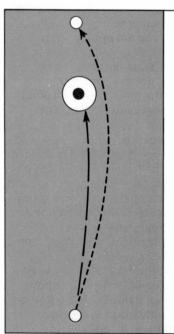

Fig 9.2. Putting is mainly about speed. Here the ball was hit too hard for the borrow that was allowed. At that pace the correct line was more towards the hole.

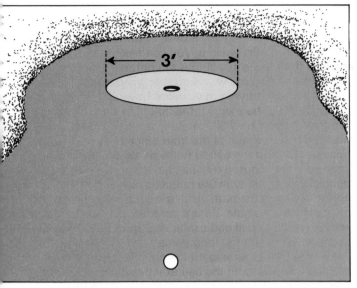

*Fig 9.3. Your putting may improve by imagining
you are putting into a 3-foot circle around the hole.*

yourself the opportunity of knowing whether the ball should
be played straight at the hole, or whether you should allow,
say, six inches borrow on the right, you are probably not
proficient enough yet to worry that it should have been
five-and-a-half inches on the right! Your aim is to avoid
three-putting, and to be sufficiently positive to single-putt
more often. So avoid slow play on the greens, but by taking
enough time, you will undoubtedly take fewer putts and
ultimately less time.

Good putting is firstly about correct reading of greens, and
then the strength of the putt. Once you have read the borrow,
concentrate on how hard to hit the ball. If you read a putt on
the right lip, but hit it too hard, it will not take the borrow, and
the putt will miss on the right. The correct *line* for that *speed*
is straight at the hole (Fig 9.2). The way to become a good
depth putter is to practise those longer putts, which most
golfers seldom do. On the course it may help you to imagine
rolling the ball into a three foot circle around the hole (Fig
9.3). I personally do not use this method, because I always
like to imagine the ball rolling into the hole. no matter how
long the putt. This, of course, is an unrealistic expectation on
some putts, but I feel that it is certainly the more positive
approach for the better putter. However, if your results

improve by thinking of the three-foot circle, then so be it.

There are times to be aggressive on putts and times to be defensive. If your target is to do no worse than two-putt, then you need to plan where you would like to play your second putt from, should the first one miss. If the green is basically flat, then try to have the ball stopping about one foot beyond the hole. If the putt has left-to-right or right-to-left borrow, remember that especially in severe cases the ball will roll downhill in the last few inches (Fig. 9.4). You must allow for this when you judge the strength, but remember that the ball is better off finishing beyond and below the hole for two reasons. First, if it is not hit with enough strength to reach the hole it will not drop in (obvious really), and secondly, if it is below the hole at least you have an uphill putt remaining.

This then begs the question on whether you should attack uphill putts. These must be hit hard enough to finish just past the hole, and whilst this is easy to judge on short putts, from the 20–30 foot range this may present a problem. Realistically at this stage you may be unlikely to hole this length, so the safest thing to do is to try to leave the ball just short of the hole. This does not mean that you should be negative when you hit the putt – always strike it firmly, but not too aggressively. Remember that an uphill putt will not take as much borrow as one on the flat.

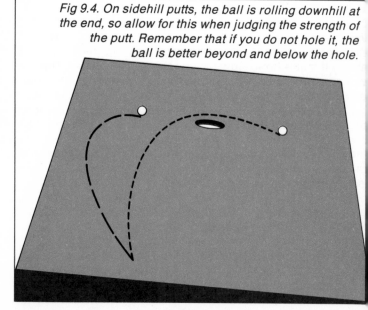

Fig 9.4. On sidehill putts, the ball is rolling downhill at the end, so allow for this when judging the strength of the putt. Remember that if you do not hole it, the ball is better beyond and below the hole.

Downhill putts, which so often have borrow as well, are the most difficult to judge. On extreme slopes, you can easily just try to set the ball rolling, only to see it finish well short of the hole leaving another downhill putt. Therefore you must try to get the ball past the hole so that your second putt is uphill. Always try to strike the putt well, rather than just timidly wafting the putter at the ball. Most right-handed golfers would prefer an uphill right-to-left putt, so try to hit the ball with sufficient pace and borrow that you have a chance of leaving yourself this putt if the ball does not go in.

Medal versus stableford and matchplay

If you have played a lot of stableford and matchplay golf, you may have become the type of golfer who is quite aggressive on the greens. By and large, this style of play suits these forms of golf, where the death or glory attitude can be beneficial, but it can become costly in medal play, where your main aim is to avoid three-putting. A later chapter has some advice on how to analyze your round, and based on this you should assess whether you putt too aggressively or too defensively. As I have already explained knowing when to attack and defend is part of the game.

Learn from others

Watch your partners putt, and by that I do not mean watch their action, but watch how fast the ball leaves the putter, and assess if that is how hard you would have hit the ball. This will give you a better chance of judging the pace and borrow of the greens. One last tip is to putt with a clean golf ball. A lump of mud or sand left on the ball is enough to send even the best hit putt off-line.

CHAPTER TEN

The positive outlook

Having explained how the technical and strategic aspects of your game should help you to break 90, it is important that you appreciate just how much the right mental attitude will contribute to that goal. To progress to your best level, the sooner you view things in a positive light, then the quicker your technical and strategic improvements will bear fruit. It has often been said that the most important six inches in golf is that between the ears! Even for those in the middle- to high-handicap range this holds true, so let us examine how that six inches can help.

Self image

It is most important that you start to develop a strong mental picture of yourself succeeding at whichever shot you are about to play. How often have you had to play a pitch shot over a bunker, had the image of fluffing the ball into it, and then fulfilled this image (Fig 10.1)? This starts a chain reaction, so that when you are faced with a similar shot again you think back to that failure and immediately have the wrong mental picture. Yes you are going to hit some poor shots – we all do – but you *must* start to build a better picture of yourself succeeding. You can even do this away from the golf course, by sitting imagining yourself on the first tee, swinging smoothly and hitting a good shot. Mentally see yourself playing the more difficult shots successfully, such as a chip over the bunker, or a three foot left-right putt for par. But do keep this mental image within the bounds of what is sensible and achievable. There is no point in thinking that just because you have *imagined* yourself carrying a ditch 250 yards in the distance, when your record for hitting a ball is only 190 yards you are suddenly going to 'find' another 60 yards. That is not reasonable or feasible. But imagining yourself crisply striking the ball to your maximum ability is what you must start to envisage.

As you look from your ball to the target, you must not ignore the hazards ahead, since they will help to determine which shot you play. Having identified the areas to avoid, you must then get a positive picture in your mind of the ball's flight. If you address the ball thinking only of where it must not go then your body will not respond as desired. You must

Fig 10.1. If you imagine failure, this will encourage bad shots.

always feed in positive thoughts and pictures. So your pre-shot routine must begin by you 'seeing' the ball's flight, then 'seeing' and feeling yourself successfully playing the shot whilst you have a practice swing. When top-class skiers, who perform leaps and somersaults as they ski downhill, wait at the top of the run for their turn, they shut their eyes, and by their movements you can see them rehearsing what they are about to perform, although their skis never leave the snow at this point. They are unable to have a proper practice at their run, so they substitute a mental rehearsal for the physical one that is not possible. We are lucky in golf that we can have both, so make the most of your practice swing and your mental preparation.

Fig 10.2. Away from the course, mentally plot your round and imagine yourself playing each hole successfully.

Seeing the round

You now know how to plot your way around the course, and you can endorse that plan by thinking about it before you play. The more vividly you can start to 'see' how you wish to play the course, the better your chances of so doing. If all you have in your mind is how badly you played last time, then you are preventing yourself from seeing success. This is especially important if there has been a particular hole or holes that have been troubling you lately. You must prevent the previous disasters from masking or clouding a new positive picture. By tackling the hole in a different manner, perhaps playing an iron from the tee instead of a wood, you will no longer view it as the hole that you just cannot play. Take time at home to sit and mentally play your round (Fig 10.2). This is especially therapeutic when bad weather or lack of time prevent you from being out on the course.

Self confidence

So many of the higher-handicap players whom I teach, seem to be apologetic for their handicap and their existence on the golf course. Anyone who plays golf does so for the enjoyment it brings, and whilst we all enjoy playing well rather than badly, it does not follow that a 3-handicap player gets more enjoyment from the game than a 23 handicap. Neither does it make the former a better person or super-human – he has simply learnt the art of getting the ball round the course. We all have to start somewhere; very few people break 90 in their first round of golf, and some never achieve that target but still enjoy the game. So do not go out on to the golf course thinking that you should not be there – it is your hobby and you have paid your green fee, so enjoy it.

Most golfers are interested only in their own game and are not really concerned about what other golfers are doing. You may feel that all eyes are upon you on the first tee, and it might be true in this instance, but once you have got off the first tee, no-one will be bothered about how you are playing. You may watch others on the first tee, but when your round begins you are too concerned with your own game to worry about them. You do not have to forget that others exist – they certainly do – and by mending pitch marks, raking bunkers and calling faster players through, we give other golfers a fair chance to play well. However, do not be over-anxious about playing whilst others watch, and do not worry about what other people may think of your golf. If you have chosen to play short of a ditch when your partners have gone for the carry, do not worry if they make detrimental remarks about your defensive play. You must stick to your game plan.

Try to become a confident player, and get used to thinking in a positive manner. Walk down the fairway with your head up, even after a bad shot. By letting your head drop and by slouching you will not develop the best frame of mind for the next shot. Even if you are playing badly and breaking 90 seems out of the question, do not waste the rest of the round; try to learn something from it that will help you in the future. The sooner you learn to cope with, and recover from, playing badly, then the better your chance of *consistently* breaking 90. In trying to develop a more confident manner, it is important to repeat positive thoughts to yourself, but I would discourage you from getting over-confident and starting to boast about how good you have become. Outwardly boastful golfers tend to get brought back down to earth.

CHAPTER ELEVEN

Why where you play affects your play

So many golfers can hit the ball better at the driving range or practice gound than on the golf course. This is not difficult to understand; at each of the first two venues there is no pressure to score, you have the luxury of hitting shot after shot, and there are no hazards. If you find that your golf in a practice situation is far superior to that on the course, then by changing your mental approach you can maintain that higher standard on the course, too.

When you practise the chances are that you will be in a relaxed state, so that your muscles are able to perform to their maximum efficiency. When you play, relaxation is harder to achieve, but you can learn to control your muscles. On the practice ground, hit some shots with a grip that is tighter than normal. You will find that your arm and shoulder muscles will start to feel tense, and the swing will not be very fluid. Next start with a tight grip, but relax your hands just prior to your backswing. The grip should be firm but relaxed, and this will help to ease your arm and shoulder muscles also. By practising tensing and then relaxing in this manner, you can use the same technique on the course to great effect. It is also very relaxing to breathe deeply, taking one deep breath and exhaling just prior to the backswing.

I once sat on the practice ground at the British Open, and watched one of the world's top professionals have his caddy call out different hole numbers to him, and he would then hit the appropriate shaped tee shot. This is the next step for you. On the practice ground imagine yourself out on the course, perhaps at the first hole, where most people get tense. Picture where the hazards are as you look ahead, and where you want the ball to land; sense that there are several sets of eyes watching your every move, and imagine your friends waiting to tee off behind you. You may start to feel a little more anxious than for the your normal practice ground shot, but employ the above techniques to control this. Use your pre-shot routine, including positive imagery, and then hit the ball. By practising in this manner when the shots occur on the course, you will already have 'played' them successfully, and your confidence will grow.

The other way to approach on-course tension and lack of form during a round, is to imagine yourself in the situation

Fig 11.1. To ease on-course tension, picture a practice ground target.

where you perform best, which is usually your practice location, or even a favourite hole on the course. On the practice ground you may always aim at a yardage marker, or distant tree, so for each shot on the course just picture that object as your target (Fig 11.1). During my years as a tournament player, I carried in my mind one of the tee shots at my home club that I particularly enjoyed, and usually played successfully. In tight situations, or on days when my confidence and ability were not all that they should be, I would put myself back on that tee, and just imagine the ball flying off into the distance. I am sure that you have holes on your course, where you hit more good shots than bad. This may be because they are wide open holes with no danger lurking, so you relax and swing smoothly. Use this to your advantage and try to imagine that each hole is like these, with no dangers lurking.

Self-imposed pressure

When playing in Pro-Ams so often I hear partners announce that 'this is a difficult hole'. Instantly they are increasing the pressure on themselves, by saying that they will need to do something special in order to score well. This same attitude is not applicable to a practice situation, or even to a friendly round, where you are more casual and relaxed. If you are guilty of pronouncing shots or holes as 'difficult', then stop immediately. By using the practice ground drill already described of imagining yourself on different holes, you can start to conquer any fears. Build up a case history of successfully playing the hole, even if it is only in your mind on the practice ground, or in an armchair.

You may play a hole rather badly continually, and start to get a complex about it. The answer to this problem is to tackle the hole in a completely different manner. If the drive is particularly difficult, take a different club to your usual one, so that you can confidently get the ball on the fairway. Play subsequent shots with clubs that you can hit well, even if you just use medium and short irons. If the second shot has been landing in bunkers short of the green, from which you do not recover very well, be sure to lay up short of them so that the problem is removed. You need to regain your confidence, and to pose yourself a different set of problems on that hole, removing the original pressure.

Outside influences

Most beginners and high-handicap players are very self conscious, and often feel that they are in the way, or holding up play. Then they begin to rush round the course, giving themselves no chance of performing to their best ability. You never see top-class players quickly grab a club and hit the ball before they have had a chance to assess the situation, and take their address position in a precise manner. This, however, is what so many higher-handicap players do, and whilst I am the last person to encourage slow play, you will take more time by rushing your shots, because you will undoubtedly end up hitting more. You would not rush on the practice ground, so do not do it on the course. Learn to set up to the ball so that it becomes second nature. This you can do best indoors with a mirror to help you, so that you can check the ball position etc. Then once you are on the course, walk at a brisk pace, but give yourself time to survey the shot. Calmly select your club, and address the ball without any undue rush. Stick to your pre-shot routine, but if faster players behind are worrying you, then call them through. You need your full attention focused on the shot in hand, not on other players.

I strongly believe that to play good golf requires discipline, and if an outside influence distracts you, then you must deal with that influence. Your playing partners may distract you in some way, but do not let them affect your concentration. Once you have reached your ball, the discipline of your pre-shot routine must bring your attention back to hitting the ball and nothing else.

CHAPTER TWELVE

Keys to concentration

I am often asked, 'How can I concentrate for three to four hours during my round?' The answer is that you do not concentrate for three to four hours but for the amount of time it takes to prepare and hit each shot. You need to be in a relaxed yet controlled state of mind to play your best, and few people can concentrate at their peak for up to four hours. Golf requires an on/off concentration, so that between shots you can, and should, relax but be prepared to switch on the concentration when needed. For tee shots, start to get into your cocoon of concentration when you arrive at the tee; and for other shots, just before you reach the ball. For shots around the green, keep the concentration and alertness more constant, there is little time between shots and you should notice how your partner's ball is reacting on the green.

It is easy to forget key movements during the round, especially if one or two shots go astray. For instance, you may have been taking your club away *lower* to the ground, and then making certain that you swing through the ball. Remember that no-one hits every shot well, and if you have decided on using certain key movements for a round, then stick to them. Perhaps by using letters of the alphabet you may remember better. For instance for the two moves mentioned above you could say to yourself LT, which substitute for *low* back and hit *through*. Use letters that you can remember readily, but from personal experience I know that this method can help.

Some players respond better to thinking about one or more specific movements, while others prefer an overall swing feel. Top-class professionals employ one or two swing thoughts for as long as they work. Try to do the same, but do not allow these thoughts to prevent you swinging to a balanced finish, which, in itself, is a desirable on-course thought.

It is harder to concentrate when you are not playing well, and often you just want to complete the round as quickly as possible. Try to keep your attention on the game, because it is still good practice even if your score is above 90. Keep to the pre-shot routine, so that you at least use the round to incorporate that as a natural part of your game.

CHAPTER THIRTEEN

How the score affects your attitude

How you are scoring in your round will probably affect your attitude and your mental outlook. So many golfers start their round poorly, perhaps dropping nearly all their handicap shots in the first six holes. They then give up mentally, but often play the rest of the round in near par figures.

Most golfers fail to warm up sufficiently before they play. If top-class players need to hit practice shots to be totally on form at the first tee, then so do you. But I know that this is not realistic, and since few club golfers spend enough time warming up, expectations on the opening few holes should not be too high. That is not to say that you cannot score well, but you should not attempt shots that are difficult, or hit the driver. Give yourself a chance by playing the first three or four holes in a defensive rather than an attacking manner. If you still play them badly, do not give up – by being hard on yourself you will become miserable and will find it hard to get better. Try to have a positive outlook for the rest of the round, even if the score looks like being above the limit. If you can play some of the remaining holes well, it will have served as a lesson that you can play badly and then pick yourself up.

Score consciousness

If you are scoring well, you may be unable to cope with the prospect of a good round, especially if it is feasible that you could break 90 for the first time. For instance, you may know that you must play the last three holes in a total of 16 shots, find the pressure too great and go to pieces. If knowing your score seems to have a detrimental effect on your play, then do not add up the nine-hole total, and just tell your partners that you do not wish to know anything about your score. You will usually know if you are doing well or badly, but exactly how well may be enough to ruin the day. Fortunately I was never score conscious, by which I mean that I rarely knew my total score until I added up the card. This I believe is an advantage for most players, although there are a few people who give of their best with additional pressure. If you are scoring well, with just a few holes left to play, you may feel that you need to know exactly what you have to score to break 90, in order to know how attacking you should be. This could work in your favour if you have shots in hand, since you can play well within yourself. It may work against you if you need to attack, as the additional demands may cause you to drop more shots. Only by experience and perhaps by experimenting, will you come to any firm conclusions about the score affecting your play, and you must then base your future rounds on this evidence.

If you are playing well and then have a few bad holes, do not give up. You may play the remaining holes very well, and still reach your goal. It is important to regard each hole as a separate entity, and do not let poor form at one upset you mentally. Think back to how your swing felt during those good holes, and reflect on your mental approach at that time. You can then direct your energies towards regaining your composure, instead of wasting time berating yourself, and possibly other people. Do not lose your temper because you will take several holes to calm down, by which time too much damage will have been done. Stay in the present, do not think back to the bad shots, or bad bounces you may have had; you can do nothing about them, but you can do something about the future shots in your round. Few top professionals play perfect rounds of golf; they too will make mistakes, causing shots to be dropped. However, their ability to put these errors out of their mind is what makes a good round of golf still possible. If you play well, then drop a few shots, you are likely to become tense, and deny yourself the chance to swing in a smooth relaxed manner. I have already dealt with relaxation in some detail, but one further way to help yourself to relax is to hum a tune quietly. I can testify to its benefit – find the right tune, and it may also help you to swing more rhythmically!

CHAPTER FOURTEEN

Practical application

I walked the course with a friend of mine, who felt he hit the ball well enough, but did not think that his scores were a true reflection of his ability. What follows is an analysis of my observations of his play, and my suggestions as to how he should have tackled the course.

Hole 1, par 4, 320 yards *(Fig 14.1)*▶

Shot 1 John failed to warm up in any sense, and did not take time to plan how he would play the hole in five shots. He had no pre-shot routine, and, in his mind, a tee shot had to be hit with a driver. He should have given himself enough time for at least 10 to 20 practice swings, which, although not ideal, are better than nothing. If he had planned how to play the hole in five shots he would have known that he did not need his driver, but a 3 or 5 wood. If he had used a pre-shot routine he would have aimed better, and given himself a chance to calm down mentally and swing smoothly.

Shot 2 Playing sensibly was over-ridden by the desire for length. A 7 iron would have been a better club to use, which would have placed the ball in range of the green for the third shot. John rushed this shot too and again had no pre-shot routine.

Shot 3 The lie and situation demanded a more lofted club to be used. With the ball down in the sand, it could not be hit cleanly. The bunker face was only five feet ahead and three feet high. Again an obsession with length made John play the wrong club. He was also becoming aware of holding up players on the tee, and became anxious.

Shot 4 Again John tried to over-power the shot and had no pre-shot routine. He thumped his club back in the bag and charged off down the fairway.

Shot 5 John chose the more difficult shot, the pitch, when he could have played the easier chip and run with a 7 or 8 iron. So poor choice of shot contributed to his downfall. He seemed in a hurry to get out of the way of those following, and was already almost disinterested in his own efforts.

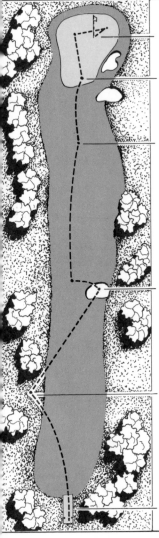

Shots 6, 7 & 8
John had 3 quick stabs at the ball, each in an uncontrolled manner.

Shot 5
A short pitch shot played with a sand iron, which John hit fat.

Shot 4
John played the 5 iron again, but struck it poorly. He was now very annoyed and angry with himself.

Shot 3
The ball was sitting down a little in the sand and John hit a 5 iron which caught the lip and went sideways out of the bunker.

Shot 2
The ball was nestled down in the rough. John topped a 5 wood into the right-hand bunker.

Shot 1
John rushed to the tee, and, without any practice swings, quickly grabbed his driver from the bag and duck-hooked the ball about 80 yards into the rough.

Shots 6, 7 and 8 At this point John just wanted to get out of the way and failed to look at any borrow or even have a practice putt.

Conclusion John's actions were typical of many golfers, where one bad shot led to another. On-course discipline was non-existent, as was any thought about planning the hole or a pre-shot routine. I mentioned all these points, and we proceeded to the next hole.

Hole 2, par 5, 485 yards   *(Fig 14.2)* ▶

John took my words on board, had a few easy swings beside the tee to calm himself down, and then duly thought about how he could play the hole in six shots. He then went through his pre-shot routine.

Shot 1 The extra time, thought and discipline had paid off, and having hit a good tee shot, John walked down the fairway in a more positive frame of mind.

Shot 2 John did not stick to his plan of playing short of the ditch in two. True, he had hit a better than average drive, but the lie was bare, which increased the chances of hitting the ball thin and low – not the ideal shot to carry a ditch. If the lie had been good, the extra risk might have been worth the gamble if he could have reached the green in two; but since this was beyond the realms of probability, it would have been wiser to have laid up short of the ditch with a mid-iron.

Shots 3 and 4 John picked the ball out of the ditch, and dropped it into a bad downhill lie in the rough. If he had been more aware, he could have gone back another 10 yards to a flat and even part of the fairway. It was worth losing distance for a flatter and better lie. From the poor lie, the pitch was always going to be a difficult shot to control, and he should have aimed for the middle of the green, and not have been drawn to the hole.

Shot 5 Annoyed at having ruined a good drive, plus the fact that he did not like bunker shots, John rushed this shot. In this instance he should have calmly had one or two practice swings outside the bunker and taken his time.

Shots 6, 7 and 8 Another three putts were caused by the poor bunker shot leaving John in three-putt range. If he had cleaned his ball, he might have got the first putt near enough, but a lump of sand prevented this.

Conclusion John changed his game plan on the basis of one good shot. He failed to appreciate how the lie affects the shot, and how that must dictate the shot you play. If he had known and used the rules a little better he would have had a simple shot to the green, and would have been putting for a five. He tried to compensate for a mistake by going for the pin and not the green. His on-course discipline, rather than his lack of ability, let him down.

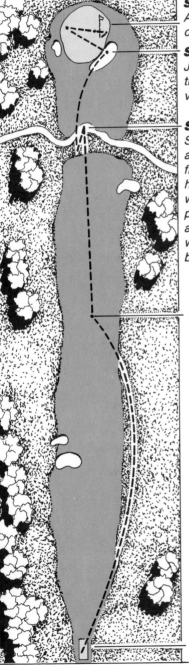

Shots 6, 7 & 8
Again John 3-putted. He did not read the green.

Shot 5
John thinned the ball from the bunker, playing in a very hurried manner.

Shots 3 & 4
Shot 3 was a penalty shot as John lifted the ball from the ditch. He then had 90 yards to the pin, with the ball lying poorly in the rough on a downhill lie. His 9 iron was pushed into the bunker and he was angry.

Shot 2
The ball was on a very bare lie, but John decided to hit his 5 wood in order to carry the ditch.

Shot 1
Using a 3 wood, John teed-up on the left of the tee, aiming right to allow his draw to bring the ball back to the fairway.

Hole 3, par 3, 150 yards (Fig 14.3)

Shot 1 The wind was quite strongly against at this hole, and John played a 5 iron, one more club than normal for the yardage. Because of the wind he decided to hit the ball hard, which sent it higher than usual. The strong wind affected it, and it landed short of the bunkers in front of the green, John should have taken a 4 or even a 3 iron, played the ball back in his stance and swung easily, thus keeping the ball lower.

Shot 2 John should have cashed in on his luck, finishing short of the bunkers and with a good lie, which meant the shot was more predictable. With the green sloping uphill, he should have kept the ball below the hole to leave an uphill putt, but his pitch shots ran well past the hole. However, he was playing the hole better than the previous two and was quite calm, positive and controlled.

Shots 3 and 4 John failed to strike the first putt with any authority. Although it was downhill, the grass was quite long and thus the ball did not roll very well. If he had hit it harder and missed, he would at least have had an uphill putt back. However, he then did well to hole the second putt, taking time to read the line.

Conclusion Club choice let John down in the first instance but, despite hitting his chip shot to a difficult spot on the green, he had still succeeded in his game plan because he had dropped only one shot. He had used a pre-shot routine on each occasion.

Summary

John made many mistakes on his first three holes. If you do not warm up, then you should not attack the course too early in the round. Instead, give your body a few holes to get going. The professional uses the practice ground to rid himself of the bad shots, and to practise any that he feels will be demanded of him that day: for example, hitting low shots into the wind. If you do not warm up sufficiently, you are less likely to strike all your early shots well, but you must get your brain working instantly, so that you do not squander and fritter shots away by bad thinking.

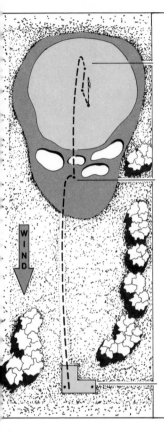

Shots 3 & 4
The first putt finished 3 feet short of the hole, but John did well to hole the next putt.

Shot 2
The ball was sitting well in short rough, John hit a wedge, and the ball finished past the pin.

Shot 1
Because of a strong wind against, John took a 5 instead of his usual 6 iron for the distance. The ball finished short of the bunkers.

Analyze your rounds

By keeping a record or chart of your rounds, you will inevitably discover facts and patterns in your play that may be very helpful in lowering your scores. It is all too easy to misinterpret the cause of high scoring, and unless you get to the root cause of the trouble, you may never play to your best ability. Either during your round, or as soon as possible afterwards, make a careful note of how you played each hole, stating the club used and where the ball finished (Fig 14.4). It would also be helpful, although perhaps a little more time-consuming, to note your mental preparation and outlook on each shot – for instance, did you stick to your pre-shot routine and aim correctly; were you still thinking about a previous shot?

It is always easy to blame a poor round on bad putting, but

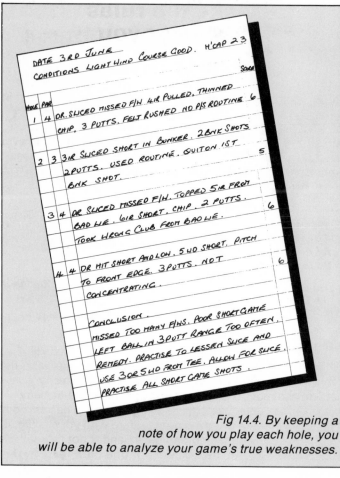

DATE 3RD JUNE
CONDITIONS LIGHT WIND COURSE GOOD. H'CAP 23

SCORE

HOLE	PAR		SCORE
1	4	DR. SLICED MISSED F/W 4IR PULLED, THINNED CHIP, 3 PUTTS, FELT RUSHED NO P/S ROUTINE	6
2	3	3IR SLICED SHORT IN BUNKER. 2 BNK SHOTS 2 PUTTS. USED ROUTINE. QUIT ON 1ST BNK SHOT.	5
3	4	DR SLICED MISSED F/W. TOPPED 5IR FROM BAD LIE. 6IR SHORT. CHIP. 2 PUTTS. TOOK WRONG CLUB FROM BAD LIE.	6
4	4	DR HIT SHORT AND LOW. 5 WD SHORT. PITCH TO FRONT EDGE. 3 PUTTS. NOT CONCENTRATING.	6

CONCLUSION.
MISSED TOO MANY F/WS. POOR SHORT GAME.
LEFT BALL IN 3 PUTT RANGE TOO OFTEN.
REMEDY. PRACTISE TO LESSEN SLICE AND
USE 3 OR 5 WD FROM TEE. ALLOW FOR SLICE.
PRACTISE ALL SHORT GAME SHOTS.

Fig 14.4. By keeping a note of how you play each hole, you will be able to analyze your game's true weaknesses.

if you put the ball in three-putt range all the time, you will certainly take three putts quite often. Hit the ball to 20 feet or less, and you will take fewer putts. So you might find that it is poor iron play that is putting extra strain on your putting. In turn, it could be bad driving that put extra strain on your iron shots, so you can see that a detailed and *honest* analysis of your round will help.

You may also discover that in certain situations, perhaps in deep rough or in the trees, you take too many shots to get the ball back into play which would indicate that your recovery shots need practising. You can then tailor your practice time to become more beneficial so that you practise the shots that are weakest.

Make the rules work for you

To the beginner and high-handicap player, the rules of golf, which are drawn up by the Royal and Ancient Golf Club of St Andrews and the United States Golf Association, seem very complicated. Whenever possible read the rule book, because being able to find the appropriate rule quickly will prevent you getting flustered and making costly mistakes. Try to become familiar with where to find those most commonly used, which are probably:

Obstructions – Rule 24.
Abnormal Ground Conditions – Rule 25.
Water Hazards – Rule 26.
Ball Lost or Out of Bounds – Rule 27.
Ball Unplayable – Rule 28.

You do not need to know a rule by heart – carry a rule book to help you. But by knowing how to use the rules they can work in your favour, and you should avoid undue penalty shots. There are endless examples of the rules I could give, but two are worth explaining:

1 A ball lies close to a staked tree, which is considered by the club as an immovable obstruction (Rule 24.2), which means that you can move the ball **without penalty**. What many golfers fail to appreciate is that having found the nearest point of relief, so that the tree does not interfere with your swing, is not in a hazard or on the putting green, and is not nearer the hole, you should drop the ball **within one club length of that point**. The ball may then roll up to two club lengths from where it first hit the ground. In some cases this may mean that you play from the fairway and not the rough. This is quite legal and your good fortune (Fig 15.1). To help you, use three pegs to mark the original position of the ball, the nearest point of relief, and one club length from that point.

2 A ball rolls into a lateral water hazard. Under Rule 26.1 a, b & c, you have five options (Fig 15.2):
1) Play it as it lies. This is seldom chosen for obvious reasons, but if a ditch is dry and you do play the shot, remember not to ground your club.
2) Stroke and distance. If you have hit the ball 200 yards, this is not a popular choice, but if the ball has not travelled very far, this could be the best option.

Fig 15.1. When dropping from a staked tree. Find nearest point of relief, drop the ball within one club length of that point. The ball may then roll a further two club lengths away, meaning that in some cases you could play from the fairway even if the ball was in the rough.

STAKED TREE

NEAREST POINT OF RELIEF

BALL

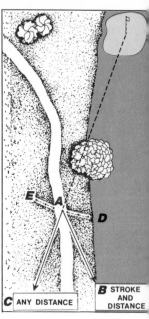

E   A

D

C ANY DISTANCE

B STROKE AND DISTANCE

Fig 15.2. Right: If the ball goes in a lateral water hazard, there are 5 options: **A** Play it as it lies. **B** Play from where the original shot was played adding one shot penalty. **C** Adding penalty shot, drop the ball any distance behind hazard keeping the point where the ball last crossed the margin of the hazard between you and the hole. **D** & **E** Adding a penalty shot, drop two clubs' lengths either side of the hazard opposite the point where the ball last crossed its margin. If was not in deep rough, E would offer the best shot.

(3) Adding a penalty shot, drop the ball behind the hazard, keeping the point where the ball last crossed the margin of the hazard between you and the hole, with no limit on how far behind the hazard the ball is dropped.

(4 & 5) Adding a penalty shot, on *either side of the hazard*, drop the ball within two club's lengths of where it last crossed the margin of the hazard, not nearer the hole. This option is not always used to its maximum advantage, as players rarely consider playing from the far side of a ditch. On occasions this may prove beneficial.

It may take you a while to work out where it is best to drop but by keeping calm and being familiar with the full extent of the rule, you should make the right decision.